50¢

My Very Own

BIRTHDAY

A Book of
Cooking and Crafts

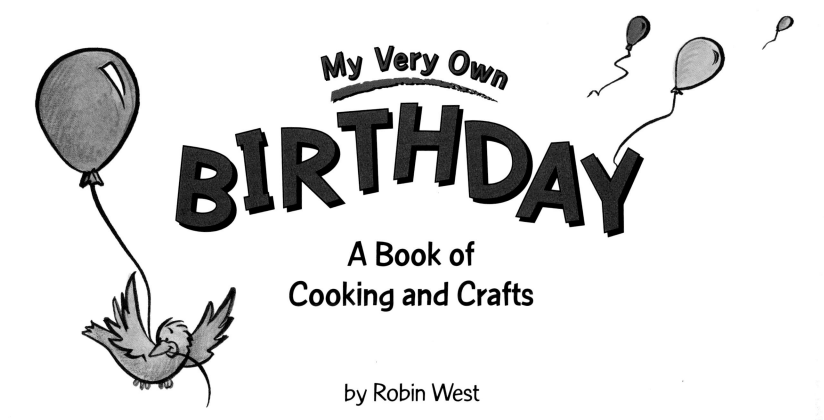

My Very Own
BIRTHDAY

A Book of
Cooking and Crafts

by Robin West

photographs by Robert L. and Diane Wolfe
illustrations by Jackie Urbanovic

Carolrhoda Books, Inc./Minneapolis

To Judy and Michael Vaughn

Carolrhoda Books, Inc. c/o The Lerner Group
241 First Avenue North, Minneapolis, MN 55401

Library of Congress Cataloging-in-Publication Data

West, Robin.
    My very own birthday : a book of cooking and crafts /
by Robin West ; photographs by Robert L. and Diane
Wolfe ; illustrations by Jackie Urbanovic.
       p.   cm. — (My very own holiday books)
    Summary: Includes ideas for creative birthday parties,
with recipes for special foods and instructions for
making invitations, decorations, favors, and more.
    ISBN 0–87614–980–8
    1. Cookery—Juvenile literature. 2. Handicraft—
Juvenile literature. 3. Children's parties—Juvenile
literature. 4. Birthdays—Juvenile literature. [1. Parties.
2. Birthdays. 3. Cookery. 4 Handicraft.] I. Wolfe, Robert
L., ill. II. Wolfe, Diane, ill. III. Urbanovic, Jackie, ill. IV.
Title. V. Series: West, Robin. My very own holiday books.
TX652.5.W45 1996
641.5'123—dc20   95–18321
                                                              CIP
                                                              AC

Manufactured in the United States of America
1 2 3 4 5 6 – H – 01 00 99 98 97 96

Contents

Birthday Greetings

It's a party! Whenever a birthday comes along it's time to sing the Happy Birthday song, play a few party games, and eat some birthday treats.

Birthdays have a way of popping up all year round, so it's never too early to begin planning your next party. Getting ready for someone's birthday (and especially for your own) can be almost as much fun as the party itself.

Start early and you'll have plenty of time to make party favors and decorations, from picture frames to place mats. With a little practice and some help from an adult friend or two, you can plan a party—complete with invitations, fun crafts, and yummy foods you've made yourself.

The ideas are endless, so begin planning now. Someone's birthday is bound to be just around the corner!

Make It Your Very Own:
How to Use This Book

RECIPES

The recipes in this book are divided into five menus, but you don't have to make a whole meal. If you are a new cook, start slowly. Choose a recipe that sounds good to you and try it. You may need lots of help at first, but be patient. The more you practice, the better you'll be.

Here are some of the easier recipes to get you started:

Fishbowl Fun
Sand Dollars
Quick-As-a-Wink Pizza
Kitty Chow

Once you know what you're doing, it's time to make a whole meal. Try one of the menus or put together your own combination.

Here are some things to consider when planning a menu:

Nutrition: Balance your menu by preparing plenty of fruit dishes, vegetables, and grains, along with smaller amounts of dairy products, meats, and other proteins. You can fill out your menu with foods that don't need recipes, such as bread, fresh fruits, raw vegetables, milk, and cheese.

Variety: Include different tastes and textures in your meal. If one food is soft and creamy, serve it with something crunchy. Salty foods taste good when served with something sweet. Try to include a variety of colors so the food is as pretty to look at as it is good to eat.

Theme: Each of the menus in this

book has a theme, just to make it more fun. Try to think up a theme of your own and choose recipes that go with it. How about a menu of foods that can be eaten with your fingers? Why not serve a birthday picnic, including Raft Rounders and Critter Cakes? Or forget about planning a meal and make a variety of desserts instead. Anything is possible!

Be sure to share your masterpiece with someone else. Whether you make one dish or an entire meal, half the fun of cooking is watching someone else enjoy the food.

CRAFTS

Like the recipes, all the crafts in this book are easy to make, but some are easier than others. If you haven't tried making crafts before, start with something easy, like some Seaside Sippers or a Galaxy-of-Stars Place Mat. As you gain confidence, put together some Pizza Pizzazz Party Invitations or a Picture-Your-Pet Frame. Once you've tackled these crafts, you'll be ready to make a Cosmic Candy Cup.

Use your imagination when decorating your crafts. Markers, colored construction paper, scraps of fabric, and glitter will give your craft a personal touch.

Cooking Smart

Whether you are a new or experienced cook, these cooking tips can help you avoid a kitchen disaster.

BEFORE YOU COOK

- Get yourself ready. If you have long hair, tie it back to keep it out of the food, away from flames, and out of your way. Roll up your sleeves and put on an apron. Be sure to wash your hands well with soap.
- Read through the entire recipe and assemble all the ingredients. It's no fun to find out halfway through a recipe that you're out of eggs.
- Go through the recipe with an adult helper and decide which steps you can perform yourself and which you'll need help with.

WHILE YOU COOK

- Raw meat and raw eggs can contain dangerous bacteria. After handling these raw foods, wash your hands and any utensils or cutting boards you've used. Never put cooked meat back on an unwashed plate that has held raw meat. Any dough that contains raw eggs isn't safe to eat until it is cooked.
- Keep cold foods in the refrigerator until you need them.
- Wash fruits and vegetables thoroughly before using them.
- Turn pot handles to the back of the stove so the pots won't be knocked off by accident. When you are taking the lid off a hot pan, always keep the opening away from your face so the steam won't burn you.

- Use a pot holder when handling hot pans. Be sure the pot holder is dry before you use it. Heat from a pan will come right through a wet pot holder.
- Always turn off the stove or oven as soon as you're done with it.
- Be careful with foods when they come out of the microwave. Although the food may seem to be cool to the touch, microwaving can produce hot spots. When you're heating a liquid in the microwave, stir it often to distribute the heat evenly.
- Only use microwave-safe dishes in the microwave. Never put anything metal in the microwave.
- Don't cut food in your hand. Use a cutting board.
- Carry knives point down.
- Be careful when opening cans. The edges of the lids are very sharp.
- Try to clean up as you go along.

AFTER YOU COOK
- Once you've finished cooking, be sure to store your creation in the refrigerator if it contains any ingredients that might spoil.
- Be a courteous cook: clean up your mess. Leave the kitchen looking as clean as (or cleaner than) you found it.

SOME CRAFTY TIPS
Assembling a craft is a lot like cooking, and many of the same tips apply. Read the instructions and gather your supplies before you start. Play it safe with your supplies, especially scissors, and be sure to get an adult friend to help you when you need it. Put down newspapers to protect your work surface. And, of course, be sure to clean up your mess when you're done.

Alien Adventure

Fantastic Flying Saucers

▼

Supersonic Soup

▼

**Banana Split
Spaceship Cake**

▼

*Cosmic Candy
Cup*

Fantastic Flying Saucers

YOU WILL NEED:

1 pound hamburger

½ cup barbecue sauce

1 tablespoon minced onion

¼ teaspoon celery seed

1 can refrigerator biscuits
(10 biscuits total)

½ cup shredded American or
Monterey Jack cheese

stuffed green and black olives

SPECIAL EQUIPMENT:
toothpicks

❶ Preheat oven to 400°. Grease muffin tins to hold 10 biscuits.

❷ Brown hamburger in skillet. Drain fat and discard.

❸ Stir in barbecue sauce, onion, and celery seed. Cook until all ingredients are warmed. Cover and remove from heat.

❹ Open canned biscuits and separate dough into 10 sections. Place one biscuit in each greased muffin cup. Press dough firmly into the cup, leaving a ¼-inch rim.

❺ Spoon the meat mixture into each cup and sprinkle with cheese.

❻ Bake for 8 to 10 minutes or until the edges of the biscuits are brown.

❼ Cool at least one minute before removing biscuits from muffin tin.

⬧ To decorate, stick one end of a toothpick in olive. Place other end of toothpick in biscuit to form spaceship landing lights. Repeat.

Makes 10

Birthday Greetings Around the Planet

How do space aliens say "Happy Birthday" to their friends? We may never know. But here's how people around our planet give their birthday greetings to each other. Pronunciations are included so you can give it a try.

German: Herzlichen Glückwunsh zum Geburtstag (HER-tslish-n glyk-vwoonsh tsoom geh-BOORTS-tahk)

Italian: Buon compleanno (BWOHN kom-pleh-AHN-oh)

Japanese: Tanjoobi omedetoo (tah-joh-bee oh-meh-deh-toh)

Norwegian: Gratulerer med dagen (gra-too-LEHR-ehr MEH DAH-gen)

Spanish: ¡Feliz cumpleaños! (feh-LEES coom-pleh-AHN-yos)

Russian: S Dnem rozhdenia (SNYOHM rohzh-DYEH-nee-ah)

Polish: Serdeczne gratulacje z okazji urodzin (sehr-DEHCH-neh grah-too-LAT-see-eh zoh-KAH-zee oo-ROH-zcheen)

Supersonic Soup

YOU WILL NEED:

1 cup finely chopped carrot

¼ cup finely chopped red pepper

¼ cup chopped onion

2 cups chicken broth

¼ cup all-purpose flour

salt and pepper to taste

2 cups milk

1 cup diced ham

1 cup shredded cheddar cheese

¼ cup sliced black olives

1 In a large saucepan, combine carrot, red pepper, onion, and broth. Bring to a boil.

2 Reduce heat. Cover and simmer until vegetables are tender, about 5 to 7 minutes.

3 In a bowl, combine flour, salt, and pepper. Gradually add milk while stirring with a whisk to avoid lumps.

4 Stir flour and milk mixture into broth and vegetables. Continue stirring and cook over medium heat until bubbly.

5 Add ham and heat until warm.

6 Ladle soup into bowls and top with small handfuls of cheese and olives.

Serves 4 to 6

BIRTHDAYS—How It All Began

People first began celebrating birthdays long before calendars were made. In ancient Egypt and Mesopotamia, people kept time by looking at the stars. With their starry calendars, Egyptians and Mesopotamians could keep track of when people were born.

Even though they knew when to celebrate, it took a long time before ordinary folks got to have birthday parties. Only the king or queen celebrated a birthday in ancient Egypt. In ancient Greece and Rome, at first only gods and emperors had birthday parties.

Early parties were huge feasts.

Both the Greeks and Romans liked to make cakes for their parties, and the Greeks added candles. (They felt that the fire showed respect for someone special.)

Those parties were so much fun that before long more and more people wanted to have their own celebrations. By the 1200s in Germany, birthday parties, candles, and cakes were commonplace. Europeans brought their birthday traditions to North America. Other immigrants brought their traditions, too. And that's why today all of us—not just kings and queens—have a special day to call our own.

Banana Split Spaceship Cake

YOU WILL NEED:

1 10¾-ounce frozen pound cake, thawed

2 cups fresh strawberries, sliced

2 cups whipped topping

1 medium banana

licorice, gumdrops, and other candies

½ cup chopped nuts

SPECIAL EQUIPMENT:
1 plastic egg-shaped panty hose container (optional)

red and orange paper streamers (optional)

❶ Slice pound cake into three horizontal layers. Place bottom layer on serving dish and cover with one-third of strawberry slices. Cover with one-third of whipped topping.

❷ Add second layer of cake and repeat. Add last layer of cake and repeat again.

❸ Peel banana and slice in half lengthwise. Use remaining whipped topping to "glue" banana slices to sides of cake. Decorate spaceship cake with licorice, gumdrops, and other candies. Sprinkle with chopped nuts.

❹ If desired, open egg-shaped panty hose container and place one half at one end of cake to form the spaceship's cone. Place other half at opposite end to form the ship's exhaust. Use paper for flames.

Serves 10

Cosmic Candy Cup

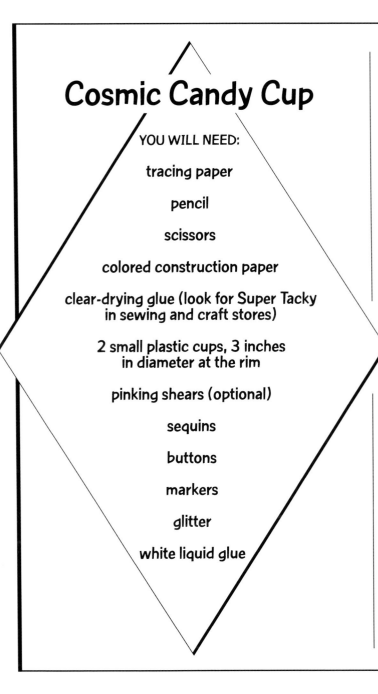

YOU WILL NEED:

tracing paper

pencil

scissors

colored construction paper

clear-drying glue (look for Super Tacky
in sewing and craft stores)

2 small plastic cups, 3 inches
in diameter at the rim

pinking shears (optional)

sequins

buttons

markers

glitter

white liquid glue

1 Place tracing paper on top of figure A on page 21. Use a pencil to trace. Cut out tracing paper pattern.

2 Place pattern on colored construction paper and trace around it. Cut out this construction paper ring. Set aside inner paper circle formed when cutting ring. Repeat, cutting a second ring from a different color of construction paper. Set one ring aside.

◆ Using clear-drying glue, attach one paper ring to the rim of a plastic cup.

◆ On the second paper ring, draw evenly spaced lines, about ¼ inch apart and about ½ inch long, leading from the inside of the ring toward the outside. Cut along these lines, and bend the paper back at a 90° angle to form tabs.

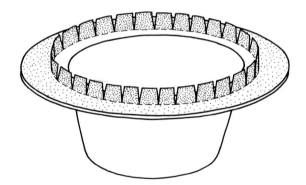

◆ Glue this ring, tabs pointing up, to the ring already attached to the cup.

◆ Using scissors or pinking shears, cut a thin strip, about ½ inch wide and 10 inches long, from colored construction paper. Attach the strip to the tabs with clear-drying glue. Glue the strip to the tabs, a few tabs at a time, as shown, giving glue time to set. The remaining plastic cup will fit inside this paper rim.

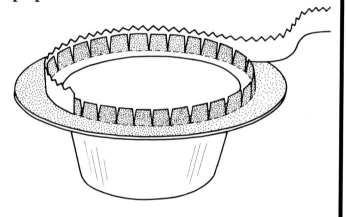

◆ To complete the first cup, take one of the left-over paper circles and glue it to the bottom of the cup. This will become the base for your candy cup.

◈ To decorate, cut out and attach paper strips, paper circles, sequins, buttons, and other items. Draw on your cup with markers or sprinkle glitter onto droplets of white liquid glue. The wilder your decorations the better for this cosmic candy cup! Decorate the second cup to match.

◈ Fill the first cup with candy and fit the second cup on top to cover.

Note: By varying the decorations, you can use this candy cup assembly for any party theme.

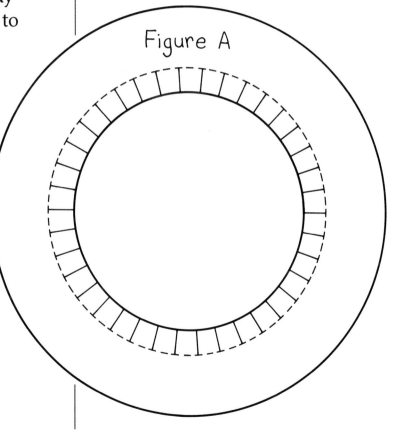

Figure A

By the Sea

Fishbowl Fun

▼

Raft Rounders

▼

Sand Dollars

▼

High Seas Slush

▼

Sand Buckets

▼

Seaside Sippers

Fishbowl Fun

YOU WILL NEED:

2 6-ounce bags plain goldfish crackers

1 6-ounce bag cheddar goldfish crackers

1 6-ounce bag pretzel goldfish crackers

1 cup pecan halves

1 cup oat cereal, such as Cheerios

1/2 cup butter or margarine, melted

1 teaspoon Worcestershire sauce

1 2-ounce envelope ranch style salad dressing mix

❶ Preheat oven to 250°.

❷ In a large bowl, combine crackers, pecans, and Cheerios.

❸ In a smaller bowl, combine butter, Worcestershire sauce, and salad dressing mix. Pour over cracker mixture and stir gently to coat.

❹ Spread mixture onto lightly greased cookie sheet. Bake 50 minutes, removing from oven every 15 minutes to stir.

❺ Spread on paper towels to cool. Serve in a fishbowl.

Makes 7 cups

Go Fish!

Did you ever think you could fish at home? You can, and it's a great thing to do at birthday parties. You can play a fun fishing game, without worms or a pole, as long as you have a deck of 52 cards (without the jokers). To play Go Fish, you'll need at least two players. Give five cards to each player, so that no one can see anybody else's cards. Put the rest of the cards facedown in a pile.

For this game, you need to find pairs of cards. A pair is two cards of the same kind, such as two queens or two eights. First, look through the cards in your hand to see if you have any pairs. Put down the pairs in front of you. The cards you have left should not match.

One player starts the game by asking another person for a card, to make a pair. For example, if you are starting and you need a six, you'll ask another player, "Do you have a six?" If the player you've asked does have a matching card, you get to keep it! Put down your new pair so everyone can see it. You can keep asking for cards as long as you keep ending up with pairs.

If the player you ask *doesn't* have a matching card, he or she will tell you to "Go fish!" Then you've got to pick up a card from the center. If the card matches something in your hand, you can put the pair down and ask again. If the card you pick up doesn't match anything, you have to keep it. (You have to stop asking for cards too.) The person on your left gets to ask next. Keep playing until all the cards jumbled in the middle are gone. The winner is the player who has "caught" the most pairs.

Raft Rounders

YOU WILL NEED:

4 ounces herbed cream cheese

1 teaspoon mayonnaise

4 large flour tortillas

4 large, thin slices cooked ham

4 large, thin slices Swiss cheese

$1/3$ cup green olives, sliced

1 large tomato, thinly sliced

$3/4$ cup shredded lettuce

8 slices process
American cheese,
cut in half

SPECIAL EQUIPMENT:
toothpicks

❶ Mix cream cheese and mayonnaise together in a small bowl. Divide into 4 equal mounds and spread evenly onto flour tortillas.

❷ Layer ham, Swiss cheese, olives, and tomato on top of cream cheese mixture. Leave uncovered about 2 inches at one end of each tortilla.

❸ Roll tortillas tightly. Cover securely with plastic wrap and refrigerate for $1/2$ hour or more.

❹ Cover serving dish with shredded lettuce "waves." Unwrap tortillas and, using a sharp knife, cut off ends and discard. Slice remaining tortilla into 4 equal lengths. Place rolled tortilla pieces on top of lettuce. Top each tortilla raft with a cheese sail on a toothpick mast.

Makes 16

Sand Dollars

YOU WILL NEED:

¼ cup plain yogurt

½ teaspoon almond extract

1 cup ground pecans

½ pound shredded coconut

2 ripe bananas, peeled and cut into ¼-inch thick rounds

1 In a bowl, combine yogurt and almond extract. Set aside.

2 Place ground pecans and coconut in separate bowls.

3 Spear a banana slice with a fork and dip the round into the yogurt mixture. Dip next into either pecans or coconut.

4 Place on a cookie sheet and remove fork. Repeat until all slices have been covered.

5 Cover cookie sheet with plastic wrap. Place in freezer for at least 15 minutes. Serve immediately or transfer to plastic bags and store in freezer.

Makes about 20

High Seas Slush

YOU WILL NEED:

1 10-ounce package frozen raspberries, slightly thawed

1 6-ounce can frozen orange-pineapple juice concentrate

2 ½ cups carbonated lemon-lime soda, chilled

❶ In blender, combine raspberries and orange-pineapple juice concentrate. Blend until slushy.

❷ Pour into 6 tall glasses. Slowly pour lemon-lime drink down the insides of each glass, over the slush.

❸ Stir gently with an up-and-down motion. Insert Seaside Sippers (see page 30) and serve immediately.

Serves 6

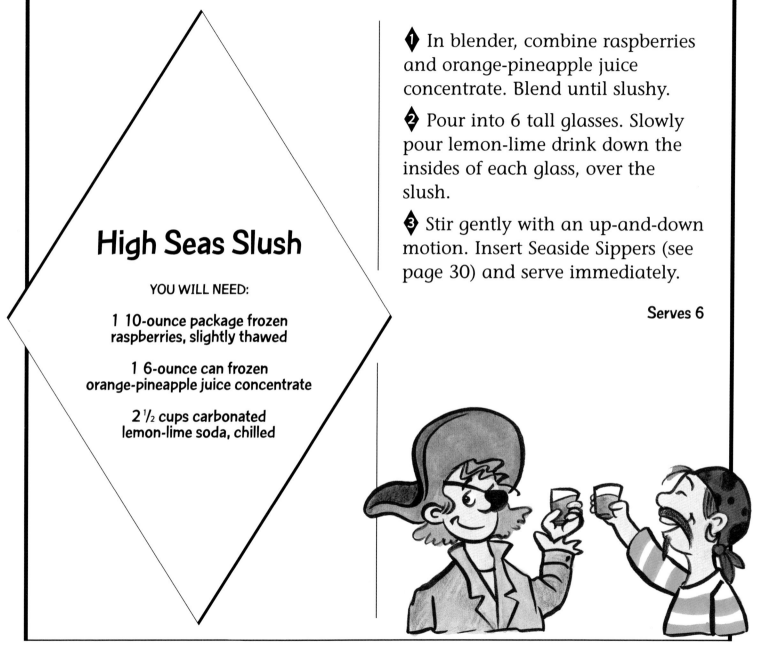

Sand Buckets

YOU WILL NEED:

¼ cup butter or margarine, softened at room temperature

1 cup confectioners' sugar

1 8-ounce package cream cheese, softened at room temperature

3⅓ cups milk

2 3½-ounce packages instant French vanilla pudding

1 cup whipped topping

½ cup mini chocolate chips

1 20-ounce bag Oreos, well crushed

red licorice whips

SPECIAL EQUIPMENT:
12 small paper cups

❶ In a large bowl, cream together butter, confectioners' sugar, and cream cheese.

❷ In another bowl, mix together milk, instant pudding, and whipped topping. Stir well to avoid lumps. Add chocolate chips and stir again to mix.

❸ Combine two mixtures.

❹ In each small paper cup, alternate layers of mixture and crushed cookies, ending with a layer of cookie crumbs.

❺ Cut licorice whips into 4-inch lengths and insert into buckets to form handles.

❻ Refrigerate for 1 to 2 hours, or freeze for 30 minutes or more to chill. Serve with a plastic spoon "shovel."

Makes 12 to 15

Seaside Sippers

YOU WILL NEED:

tracing paper

pencil

scissors

colored construction paper

paper punch

markers

glitter

sequins

white liquid glue

drinking straws

❶ Seaside sippers slip over your straw to make any drink special. Draw your own sipper shape or use one of the patterns on pages 32 and 33. When creating your own sipper shape, make sure it is no wider than 4½ inches and no taller than 6 inches. Skip to step 4 if you are making your own shape. If you plan to use one of the patterns, follow steps 2 and 3.

2 Place tracing paper on top of desired shape on page 32 or 33, and trace. Cut out tracing paper pattern.

3 Place pattern on colored construction paper and trace around it. Cut out shape.

4 Use a paper punch to make two holes in your shape. One should be at least 1/2 inch from the top of the shape. The other should be at least 1/2 inch from the bottom.

5 Decorate the shape using colored construction paper, markers, glitter, sequins, and glue.

6 Insert straw through holes as shown.

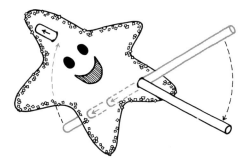

Note: Straw covers can be made to fit any party theme. For example, for a Purrfect Pet Party, create dog, cat, canary, and mice sipper shapes.

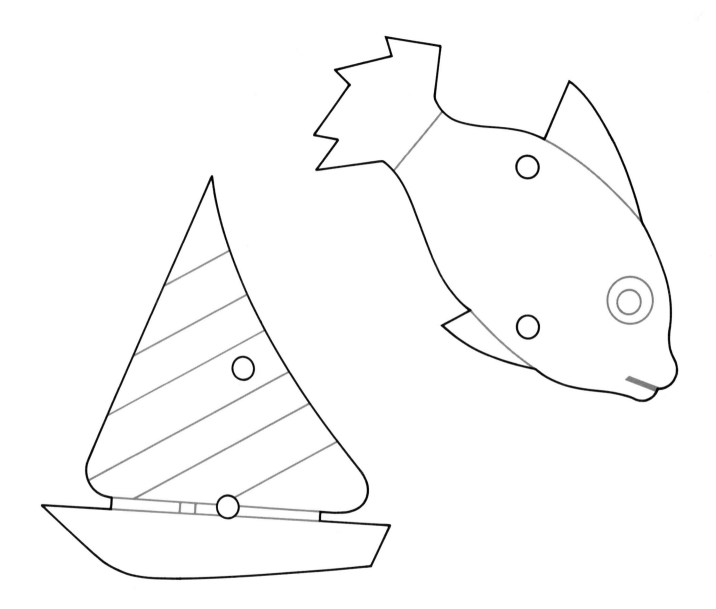

Pizza Party

Quick-As-a-Wink Pizza

▼

Eye-Opener Fruit Bowls

▼

Sweet Dreams Pizza

▼

*Pizza Pizzazz
Party Invitation*

Quick-As-a-Wink Pizza

YOU WILL NEED:

4 6-inch prebaked
pizza crusts

1 14-ounce jar pizza sauce

SUGGESTED TOPPINGS:
pepperoni slices

shredded mozzarella cheese

grated Parmesan cheese

black or green olives

Italian sausage, cooked and sliced

hamburger, cooked and crumbled

green or red pepper strips

mushrooms, sliced

onion, cut into rings
or chopped

❶ Preheat oven to 450°.

❷ Place prepared pizza crusts on cookie sheet. Spread pizza sauce onto crusts.

❸ Cover pizzas with desired toppings.

❹ Bake for 10 to 15 minutes or until cheese is melted and bubbly.

Serves 4

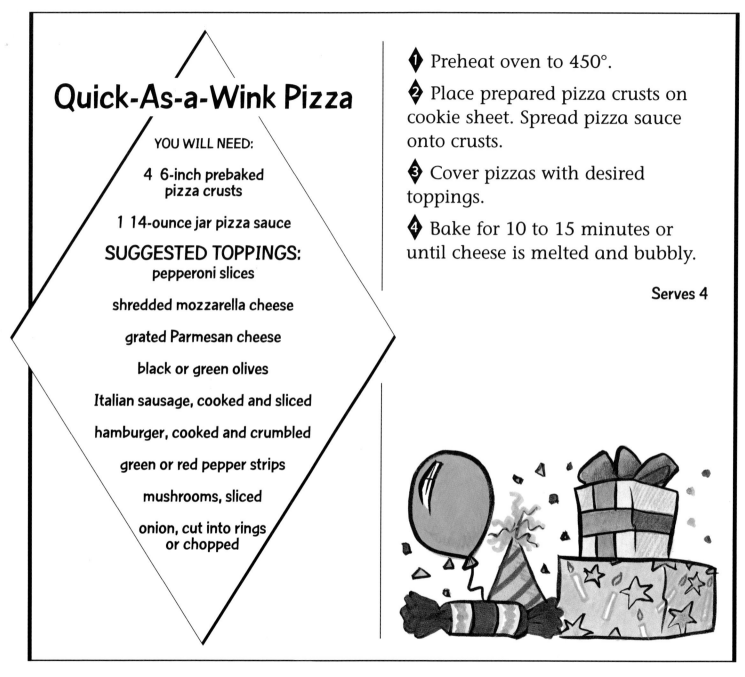

Birthday Sharing

Do you share a birthday with somebody famous? Lots of people do. If you were born on February 17, you share a birthday with Michael Jordan. If July 24 is your big day, then Amelia Earhart is your birthday twin.

Sharing a birthday can be fun. If your birthday twin is a living person, try sending him or her a card. Be sure to mention that it's your birthday too.

Not all of us want to share our birthdays all the time, however. For 14 years, Miss Annie Ide had been a birthday twin with someone very well known—Jesus Christ. Being born on Christmas meant that Annie never felt like she had a birthday of her very own.

When a family friend heard of Annie's problem, he gave her a very unusual gift.

In 1891, Mr. Robert Louis Stevenson gave Miss Annie Ide *his* birthday. It was on November 13, when no one particularly famous had been born.

Since Mr. Stevenson was both a writer and a lawyer, he drew up a legal-sounding declaration: "I, Robert Louis Stevenson . . . being in sound mind, and pretty well, I thank you, in body: In consideration that Miss Annie H. Ide . . . was born out of all reason upon Christmas Day . . . I have transferred . . . to the said Annie H. Ide, all and whole my rights and privileges in the thirteenth day of November, formerly my birthday."

Annie very happily celebrated her birthday on November 13 for the rest of her life.

I'M GLAD TO SHARE IT.

HAPPY BIRTHDAY

Eye-Opener Fruit Bowls

YOU WILL NEED:

4 oranges

3 bananas, peeled and sliced

1 cup fresh strawberries, cut in half

1 cup seedless grapes

1/2 cup sour cream

1 tablespoon honey

1 tablespoon orange juice

2 tablespoons brown sugar

❶ Cut oranges in half. Use a spoon to dig out orange sections, without tearing the peel. Save empty orange peels to use as salad bowls.

❷ Separate orange sections and remove seeds and membrane.

❸ In a large bowl, combine orange sections with bananas, strawberries, and grapes.

❹ Combine sour cream, honey, and orange juice in a small bowl. Pour over fruit, tossing to coat fruit well with sour cream mixture.

❺ Spoon fruit into orange peel bowls. Sprinkle with brown sugar.

Note: Fruit bowls can be prepared before the party and refrigerated.

Makes 8

Sweet Dreams Pizza

YOU WILL NEED:

peanut oil or cooking spray

$\frac{1}{4}$ cup butter or margarine

6 cups miniature marshmallows

6 cups oat cereal, such as Cheerios

1 cup peanut butter

$\frac{3}{4}$ cup chopped peanuts

$\frac{3}{4}$ cup chocolate chips

$\frac{1}{4}$ cup shredded coconut

$\frac{1}{2}$ cup raisins

1 Use peanut oil or cooking spray to grease a 12-inch pizza pan.

2 Melt butter and marshmallows. If using a stove, cook in a saucepan over low heat, stirring until melted. Remove from heat and transfer to large mixing bowl. If using a microwave, melt butter in a microwave-safe container. Add marshmallows and continue to melt, stirring frequently. Remove from microwave.

3 Add cereal to marshmallow mixture. Stir to mix.

4 Spread evenly in pizza pan. Cover with peanut butter. Then sprinkle "pizza" with peanuts, chocolate chips, coconut, and raisins.

5 Allow to cool, then cut into slices and serve.

Serves 12

Pizza Pizzazz
Party Invitation

YOU WILL NEED:

1 piece 12- by 18-inch
colored construction paper

ruler

pencil

scissors

scoring tool

1 piece 9- by 12-inch
colored construction paper

construction paper scraps

glue

THE BOX:

❶ Trim down a sheet of 12- by 18-inch construction paper to 11 by 14 inches. Place the sheet of paper on a flat surface, with a short end facing you.

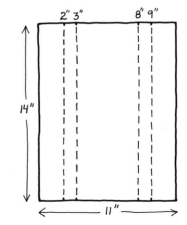

Hold your ruler along the top edge of the paper and make pencil marks at the 2-, 3-, 8-, and 9-inch points. Repeat at the bottom edge. Then use your ruler and a pencil or a scoring tool to connect the pencil marks.

2 Turn the paper 90°, so the long end faces you. Place your ruler along the top edge of the paper and make pencil marks at the 2-, 3-, 8-, and 9-inch points. Repeat at the bottom edge. Then use your ruler and a pencil or a scoring tool to connect those pencil marks.

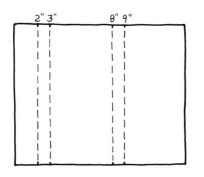

3 Using scissors, cut away the shaded areas as shown.

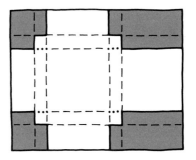

Cut again at the dotted lines to make tabs.

4 If you have not already scored the lines, do so now with a scoring tool. Fold along these lines to form the box. Decorate with paper scraps.

THE CARD:

1 Trim down a sheet of 9- by 12-inch construction paper to 5 by 10 inches. Fold this sheet in half to make a square.

2 Trim the corners of the square to make a rough circular pizza shape. Be sure not to cut through all of the folded edge.

3 Decorate the top of the pizza by gluing on construction paper scraps.

4 On the inside of the pizza card, print the name or theme for the party.

You'll also want to include the name of the person giving the party, where it will take place, and when. For more on how to write and send invitations, see the section on invitation etiquette on page 43.

TO ASSEMBLE:

Place the pizza invitation in the box and fold it shut. You can seal the box with another paper scrap and some glue.

Note: You can use the same box and card invitation for other party themes.

Invitation Etiquette

Invitations are an important part of planning a party. Without them, no one would show up!

When you are making your guest list, keep a few tips in mind. If you are inviting several people from a group of friends, why not ask them all to come? If you are throwing a party for a friend, be sure to invite people your friend knows and likes, not just people you know and like.

Once you've finished your guest list, it's time for the invitations. You'll want to send or hand deliver an invitation at least two weeks in advance.

Whether you use a printed card or one you have made, be sure to include the following information:

♦ Let people know it's your birthday. (Your guests won't know it's your special day unless you tell them.) A simple "It's my birthday!" should do just fine.
♦ Include your name.

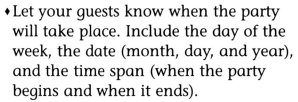

♦ Let your guests know when the party will take place. Include the day of the week, the date (month, day, and year), and the time span (when the party begins and when it ends).
♦ Include the address of the place where the party will be held and the phone number.
♦ Give your guests an idea of what to wear or bring along. If you are having a beach birthday party, remind your guests to bring a swimsuit and lotion.
♦ You may want the people you've invited to let you know, in advance, if they can come. On many printed invitations, you will find the letters R.S.V.P. at the bottom. This is an abbreviation for the French phrase *"Répondez s'il vous plaît."* That means "Reply if you please." If you put R.S.V.P. on your invitation, your guests will know to contact you in advance.

A Purrfect
Pet Party

Cheesy Corn Pups

▼

Bunny Slaw

▼

Kitty Chow

▼

Critter Cakes

▼

*Picture-Your-Pet
Frame*

Cheesy Corn Pups

YOU WILL NEED:

8 hot dogs

2 process American cheese slices,
cut into 8 long, narrow strips

1 11½-ounce can refrigerated
corn bread twists
(8 twists total)

1 tablespoon butter or margarine, melted

1 tablespoon sesame seeds

SPECIAL EQUIPMENT:
8 bamboo skewers

❶ Preheat oven to 375°. Place skewers in water to soak.

❷ Using a sharp knife, cut a slit lengthwise down each hot dog. Leave 1½ inches unslit at one end.

❸ Insert a cheese strip into each slit. Insert a soaked wooden skewer into each hot dog at the unslit end.

❹ Open and unroll refrigerated corn bread twists. Separate dough into 8 equal pieces. Start at the cut end of each hot dog and wrap dough around hot dog to cover cheese completely. Press ends of dough together to seal.

❺ Place on ungreased cookie sheet, cheese side up. Brush with melted butter and sprinkle with sesame seeds.

❻ Bake for 12 to 15 minutes or until corn bread is golden brown.

Makes 8

Bunny Slaw

YOU WILL NEED:

2 cups shredded carrots

1 red apple, cored and chopped

$\frac{1}{3}$ cup raisins

2 tablespoons plain yogurt

1 tablespoon maple syrup

1 cup seedless grapes

1 small carrot, cut into long, narrow strips

1 In a medium bowl, combine carrots, apple, and raisins.

2 In a small bowl, combine yogurt and maple syrup.

3 Add yogurt dressing to carrot mixture and toss until moistened.

4 Spoon into small serving bowls. Decorate with grapes and carrot strips to make rabbit eyes, ears, and whiskers. Cover and chill before serving.

Serves 6

Kitty Chow

YOU WILL NEED:

1 12-ounce box honey graham cracker cereal

1 15-ounce box raisins

1 10-ounce can mixed nuts

1 12-ounce package chocolate chips

1 12-ounce jar creamy peanut butter

1 teaspoon vanilla extract

1 pound confectioners' sugar

SPECIAL EQUIPMENT:
large plastic bag

colored plastic wrap

ribbon or
licorice whips

❶ In a large bowl, combine cereal, raisins, and nuts.

❷ In a microwave-safe container, place chocolate chips and peanut butter. Melt them together in a microwave oven. Stir in vanilla and blend well.

❸ Pour peanut butter mixture over cereal mixture and stir until well coated.

❹ Put confectioners' sugar in a large plastic bag. Add cereal mixture, tie plastic bag securely shut, and shake until well coated.

❺ Place cupfuls of coated cereal mixture on squares of colored plastic wrap and tie shut with ribbon or licorice whips.

Note: Kitty Chow bags make great party favors.

Makes 16 bags

Critter Cakes

YOU WILL NEED:

1 package yellow cake mix, plus oil, milk, and eggs as required

1 can vanilla frosting

1 can chocolate frosting

gumdrops

chocolate chips

marshmallows

sprinkles

shredded coconut

❶ Prepare and bake cupcakes according to package instructions.

❷ Cool. Frost each cupcake.

❸ Use remaining ingredients to decorate the cakes to look like your favorite pet or animal.

Makes 24

Some Birthday Ideas for Your Pet

If you want your pet's birthday to be extra special, plan some fun things to do:

- Give a yummy pet food treat as a gift.
- Read one of your favorite books to your pet. (Who knows? It could end up being your pet's favorite book, too.)
- Write a play for you and your pet. Then perform it for your family and friends.
- Sing or write a song for your pet.
- Draw a picture of your pet and give it as a birthday present.
- Get some friends and their pets together and have a pet talent show.

Picture-Your-Pet Frame

YOU WILL NEED:

clear plastic lid, approximately
$4\frac{1}{2}$ inches in diameter

2 or more sheets colored construction paper

pencil

scissors

white liquid glue

tracing paper

clear-drying glue (look for
Super Tacky in fabric
and craft stores)

yarn

pet photo

FRAME BACKING:

1 Place plastic lid on colored construction paper. Use it as your pattern and trace around it. Repeat, then cut out both circles.

2 Glue circles together and allow to dry.

3 With a scissors, make two cuts about ¼ inch long at the top and bottom and at either side of the frame backing. These tabs will hold your frame backing securely against the frame front.

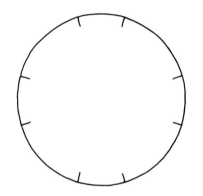

FRAME FRONT:

1 You can create your own shape for a pet picture frame or use the pattern on page 53. If you make your own shape, skip to step 4. Be sure your design is at least 5 inches high and 5 inches wide. If you use the pattern, follow steps 2 and 3.

2 Place tracing paper on top of figures B-1 through B-10 on page 53. Trace shapes with a pencil. Cut out patterns.

3 Place patterns on sheets of colored construction paper and trace around them. Cut out these construction paper shapes.

4 If you use the pattern, assemble shapes as shown. (Shaded areas should be hidden behind the muzzle, or figure B-2.) If you create your own shape, decorate the animal face by gluing on bits of colored construction paper. Make your frame look unique by adding stripes, spots, or whatever else you like.

5 Apply clear-drying glue along the top outer edge of the plastic lid. Place your paper frame facedown on a flat surface. Center the lid over your paper animal frame and press down to glue in place. Allow to dry.

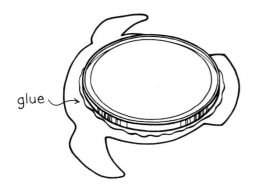

glue →

6 Cut a strand of yarn 8 to 10 inches long. Tie the yarn ends together in a bow or knot. Apply a thin line of clear-drying glue around the lid edge. Slip the yarn circle around the lid back and onto the glue. Allow to dry.

TO ASSEMBLE:

1 Position pet photo against frame backing so it will be visible through frame window. Glue photo to backing and allow to dry.

2 Bend tabs along edge of frame backing. Press photo and backing into plastic lid. Hang your pet picture frame to display.

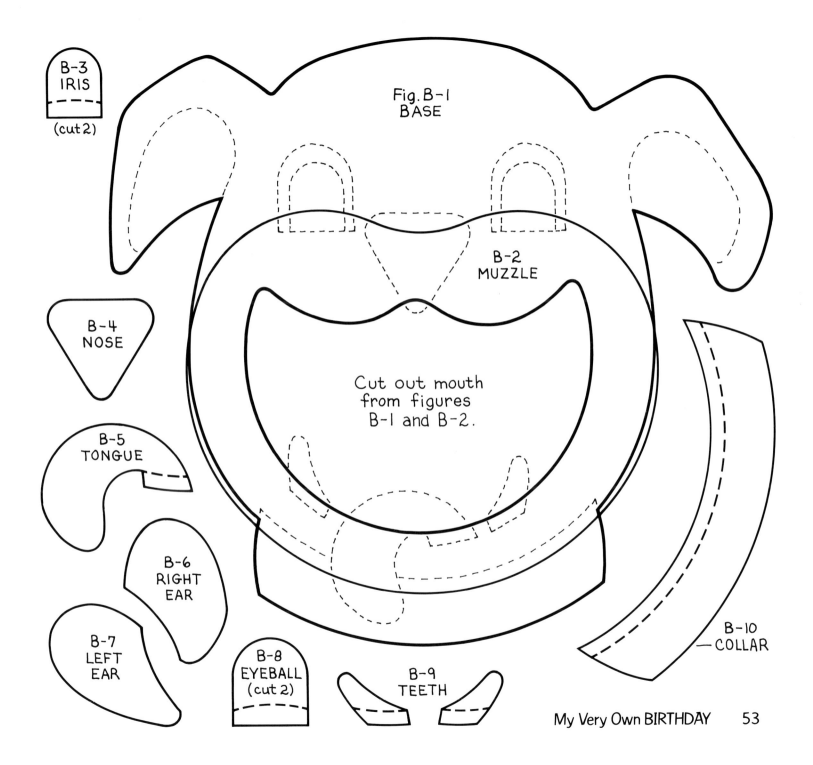

B-3
IRIS
(cut 2)

Fig. B-1
BASE

B-2
MUZZLE

B-4
NOSE

Cut out mouth
from figures
B-1 and B-2.

B-5
TONGUE

B-6
RIGHT
EAR

B-7
LEFT
EAR

B-8
EYEBALL
(cut 2)

B-9
TEETH

B-10
COLLAR

Starry, Starry Night

Cheesy Chicken Delight

▼

Dream Green Beans

▼

Heavenly Stars Salad

▼

Toasty Angel Cake

▼

*Galaxy-of-Stars
Place Mat*

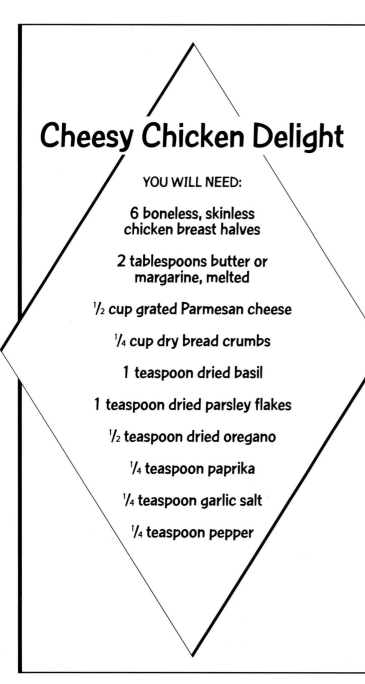

Cheesy Chicken Delight

YOU WILL NEED:

6 boneless, skinless chicken breast halves

2 tablespoons butter or margarine, melted

1/2 cup grated Parmesan cheese

1/4 cup dry bread crumbs

1 teaspoon dried basil

1 teaspoon dried parsley flakes

1/2 teaspoon dried oregano

1/4 teaspoon paprika

1/4 teaspoon garlic salt

1/4 teaspoon pepper

1 Preheat oven to 375°. Grease a 9- by 13-inch baking dish.

2 Rinse chicken pieces with water and dry on paper towels.

3 Place melted butter in shallow bowl. Combine remaining ingredients in another shallow bowl.

4 Take chicken pieces and dip first into butter, then into remaining ingredients.

5 Place in baking dish. Bake 30 minutes or until chicken is well done.

Serves 6

Dream Green Beans

YOU WILL NEED:

½ pound fresh mushrooms,
cleaned and sliced

1 tablespoon butter or margarine

1 16-ounce package frozen,
cut green beans

¼ teaspoon pepper

¼ cup shredded cheddar cheese

1 small can French fried
onion rings

❶ In a skillet, sauté mushrooms in butter.

❷ Microwave or cook beans on stove, according to package instructions.

❸ Combine beans and mushrooms. Add pepper and stir to mix lightly. Spoon mixture into 1-quart serving dish.

❹ Sprinkle cheese and onion rings on top. Serve immediately.

Serves 5

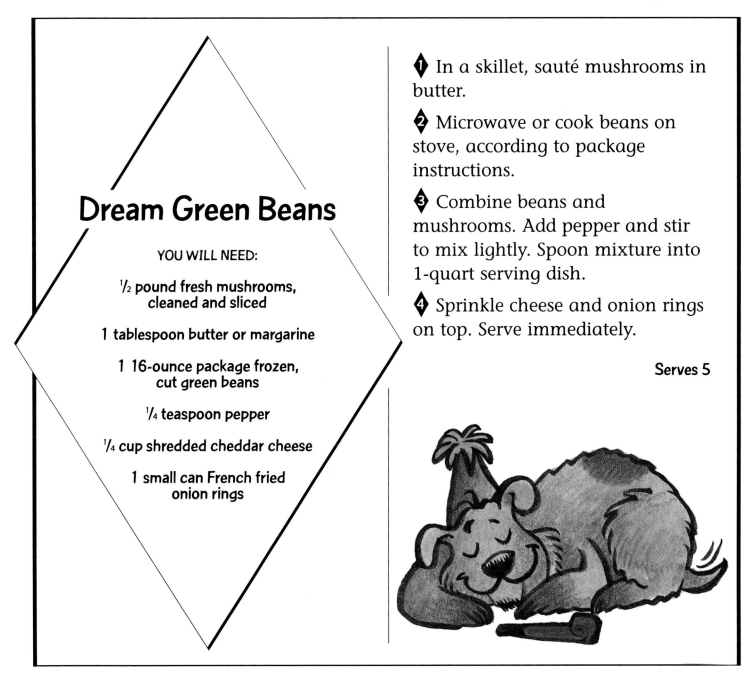

Heavenly Stars Salad

YOU WILL NEED:

4 lettuce leaves

1 cup shredded lettuce

2 pears, peeled and sliced thin

$\frac{1}{4}$ cup blue cheese, crumbled
or
$\frac{1}{2}$ cup shredded cheddar cheese

$\frac{1}{2}$ cup chopped pecans

SPECIAL EQUIPMENT:
star cookie cutter

DRESSING:
1 teaspoon raspberry or
other flavored vinegar

3 tablespoons olive oil

$\frac{1}{2}$ teaspoon sugar

❶ Mix dressing ingredients together in a bowl and set aside.

❷ Place one lettuce leaf on each salad plate. Top with shredded lettuce.

❸ Using a cookie cutter, cut star shapes from sliced pears. Place pear stars on top of lettuce.

❹ Sprinkle with cheese and nuts. Drizzle dressing over salad.

Serves 4

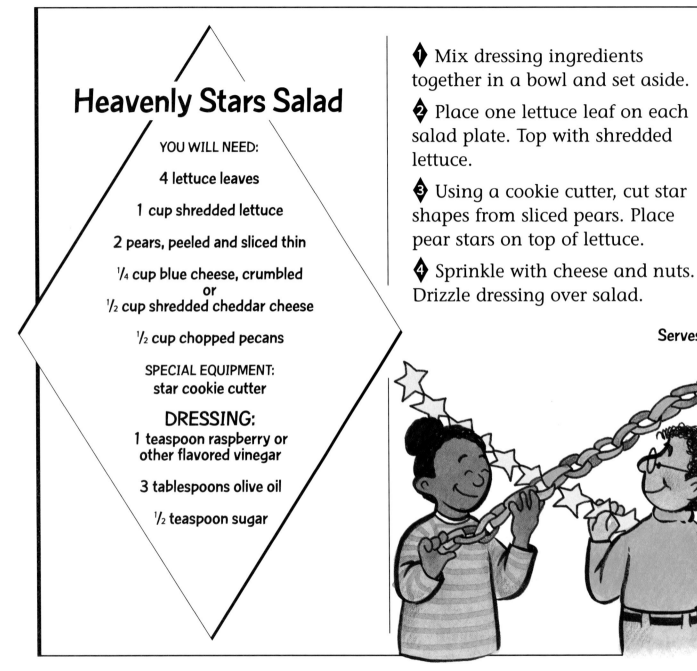

Toasty Angel Cake

YOU WILL NEED:

1 prebaked angel food loaf cake,
about 7 by 3 inches

3 cups fresh strawberries

¼ cup sugar

1 quart strawberry flavored frozen yogurt

½ cup whipped topping

❶ Cut angel food cake into 8 slices. Lightly toast the slices in a toaster or toaster oven. Place slices on individual dessert plates and allow to cool.

❷ Cut off green tops from strawberries, wash, and slice.

❸ In a small bowl, mix strawberry slices and sugar.

❹ Spoon frozen yogurt over slices of cake. Top with strawberries. Garnish with whipped topping. Serve immediately.

Serves 8

Galaxy-of-Stars Place Mat

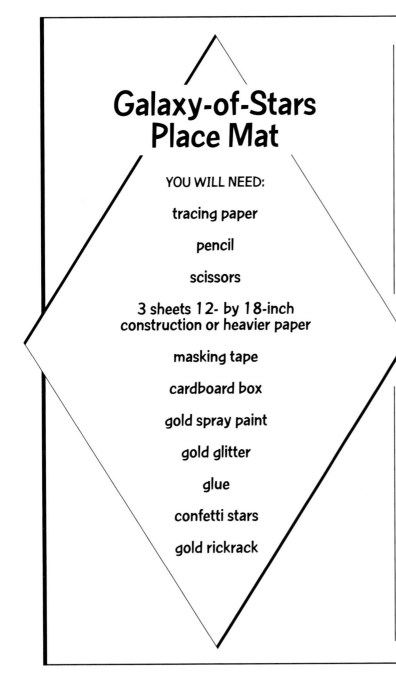

YOU WILL NEED:

tracing paper

pencil

scissors

3 sheets 12- by 18-inch
construction or heavier paper

masking tape

cardboard box

gold spray paint

gold glitter

glue

confetti stars

gold rickrack

❶ Place tracing paper on top of figures C and D on page 61. Trace around the star shapes with a pencil, and cut them out.

❷ Place both figures on top of stiff, light-colored construction paper and trace around them. Repeat several times.

❸ Cut out star shapes, being careful to cut only the shapes themselves. Use masking tape to tape together scissor cuts leading from one star shape to the next. This will be your template.

❹ Take one sheet of black or other dark colored construction paper and place it flat in the box. Put the template on top of the black sheet, lining up the edges carefully.

❺ Spray over the template lightly with gold spray paint. Hold the spray paint can carefully so no paint is sprayed outside the box.

❻ Lightly sprinkle gold glitter on the star shapes while the paint is still drying. Remove the template and set aside on old newspapers. Carefully remove place mat from box and lay it flat to dry.

❼ Repeat steps 4, 5, and 6 for each place mat. Once place mats are dry, glue colored confetti stars on top. Cut lengths of gold rickrack and glue them along the short ends of each mat.

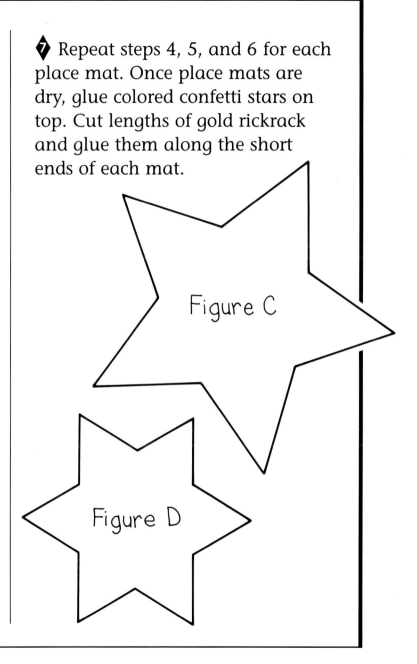

Figure C

Figure D

Recipe List

Beverage
High Seas Slush

Side Dishes and Snacks
Fishbowl Fun
Sand Dollars
Eye-Opener Fruit Bowls
Bunny Slaw
Kitty Chow
Dream Green Beans
Heavenly Stars Salad

Main Dishes
Fantastic Flying Saucers
Supersonic Soup
Raft Rounders
Quick-As-a-Wink Pizza
Cheesy Corn Pups
Cheesy Chicken Delight

Desserts
Banana Split Spaceship Cake
Sand Buckets
Sweet Dreams Pizza
Critter Cakes
Toasty Angel Cake

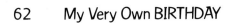

Glossary

almond extract—a liquid used to give almond flavor to food

bamboo skewer—a slender, pointed stick used to hold food in place

boil—heat a liquid until it bubbles rapidly

brown—cook food, such as hamburger, until it is light brown

chill—refrigerate until cold

core—cut out the central part of a fruit, which often contains the seeds

cream—beat several ingredients together until the mixture has a smooth consistency

drizzle—pour a thin stream of liquid over food in a random pattern

garnish—decorate with small pieces of food

grease—coat with a thin layer of butter, margarine, shortening, or cooking spray

olive oil—a clear, golden oil made from olives

paprika—a red seasoning made from the ground dried pods of the capsicum pepper

parsley—a green plant used as a garnish or to flavor food

preheat—allow oven to heat up to a certain temperature before using

sauté—fry quickly over high heat in a small amount of oil or fat, stirring to prevent burning

score—mark with a deep line or crease

shred—cut into long, ragged pieces

simmer—cook over low heat in liquid kept just below the boiling point

tortilla—a thin, round piece of bread made from corn or wheat flour

toss—combine foods by lightly lifting, turning, and dropping them with a fork

trace—copy a pattern onto another piece of paper

tracing paper—paper thin enough to see through when placed on top of a pattern

vanilla extract—a liquid used to give vanilla flavor to food

whisk—a small wire kitchen tool used for beating foods by hand

Worcestershire sauce—a strong-tasting, dark brown liquid used to flavor food

Index